Thomas C. De Leon

South Songs

from the lays of later days

Thomas C. De Leon

South Songs
from the lays of later days

ISBN/EAN: 9783337266011

Printed in Europe, USA, Canada, Australia, Japan

Cover: Foto ©Thomas Meinert / pixelio.de

More available books at **www.hansebooks.com**

South Songs:

FROM THE

LAYS OF LATER DAYS.

COLLECTED AND EDITED

BY

T. C. DE LEON.

New-York:

BLÉLOCK & Co., No. 19 BEEKMAN STREET.

1866.

TO THE

Women of Richmond,

WHOSE NOBLE SACRIFICES AND UNTIRING EXERTIONS

FOR THE SICK DURING THE WHOLE WAR,

HAVE WRITTEN THEM IN LETTERS OF LOVE,

VERITABLE SISTERS OF MERCY,

This Volume is Inscribed.

PREFACE.

A BOOK without a preface is like a salad without salt; but in offering the poems in this volume to the public, I can add little to what they speak for themselves.

The sole object of the collection is to make known a few noble poems that belong rather to the world than to any particular section, and to show those who have read REBEL RHYMES that

" *There's life in the old land yet* "

to do higher and better things.

Knowing that the South was surrounded during the war by a Chinese wall, that hid many important points of her *history* even from those beyond it, I was still surprised at the utter ignorance in the North of her having produced any thing like a high order of poetry. This ignorance extended, too, even to those whose principles or sympathies made them peer, with straining eyes, through every possible crevice in the barrier.

It is with diffidence, proportioned to the difficulties that surround it, that I have approached the task. The garland is to be gathered from a field extensive and teeming with a rank luxuriance of growth, that it must often puzzle the analyst to separate from the really valuable.

Little as is known of it, and confined, as it has ever been, to particular cliques, there is yet much latent literature in the South. The terrible friction, however, so long and so roughly applied, brought only the metrical element to the surface.

In prose of all kinds the South stood still, perhaps retro-graded; but she

" Lisped in numbers, for the numbers came !"

The thousand tragical incidents and picturesque situations of a war like this offered rare motives to the true poet, and tempting opportunities to the rhymster of low degree.

Magazines, albums, and newspaper corners overflowed with the effusions of these latter, on all subjects, and of all lengths.

But occasionally in a great crisis of the war, or when a heavy calamity bore upon the whole people, some mightier one lifted his voice and spoke words that live. These I have en-deavored to preserve in more durable form than the pressure of the times when they were uttered could allow. Some of them were comparatively unknown, even in the South; partly, that grave and absorbing duties of the hour weighed upon the public mind; but more, I imagine, from want of some general medium of circulation.

Many again found their way to the camps, were at once adopted by the soldiers, and became

" Familiar in their mouths as household words."

But, as with the popular poems of most revolutions, these were the "taking" songs of a lower order—ephemera that have lived out the day for which they were born.

In this effort to show the *quality,* and not the *quantity,* of Southern poetry, few even of the most popular of these have been introduced.

Where possible, I have had each poem carefully corrected by its author.

I have been warned that in certain quarters the poems are considered rebellious—incendiary, even—and as tending to revive a bitterness now buried and still. To these irrationals I have no word to say. I ask no favor at their hands, having sufficient confidence in my adopted children to trust them to stand alone.

If poems, born of revolution, bore no marks of the bitter need that crushed them from the hearts of their authors, they would have no value whatever, intrinsic or historical.

The feelings that prompted them live no longer. The South put her cause in the hands of the God of Battles. She has made no murmur since his decree was spoken.

A people who have accepted the inevitable with the dignified quiet of hers, can be taught no wrong by the repetition, in perfect peace, of words spoken to them while yet in the heat of a bitter struggle.

The effect of the war has been to raise the Southern character in the opinion of the North; and the feeling that the South is a conquered province—abject and bound—is fast dying out in the breadth of the land. These poems may aid in this good work; but read at every fireside in the South, they are to-day as harmless as the *"Lays of Ancient Rome."*

Their authors, whatever they may have been, are now simply private citizens. I shall not invade their *sancta* to search for the motives that impelled them. That they wrote honestly, none who read their words can doubt; and I am well content to leave them in the hands of the public, saying only :

" *By their works shall ye know them.*"

T. C. DE L.

BALTIMORE, MD., February 15, 1866.

Index of Poems and Authors.

South Songs.

SOUTH SONGS.

Your Mission.[1]

Fold away all your bright-tinted dresses,
  Turn the key on your jewels to-day,
And the wealth of your tendril-like tresses
  Braid back, in a serious way:
No more delicate gloves—no more laces,
  No more trifling in boudoir or bower;
But come—with your souls in your faces—
  To meet the stern needs of the hour!

Look around! By the torch-light unsteady,
  The dead and the dying seem one.
What! paling and trembling already,
  Before your dear mission's begun?
These wounds are more precious than ghastly;
  Time presses her lips to each scar,

As she chaunts of a glory which vastly
  Transcends all the horrors of war.

Pause here by this bedside—how mellow
  The light showers down on that brow!
Such a brave, brawny visage! Poor fellow!
  Some homestead is missing him now:
Some wife shades her eyes in the clearing,
  Some mother sits moaning, distressed,
While the loved one lies faint, but unfearing,
  With the enemy's ball in his breast.

Here's another; a lad—a mere stripling—
  Picked up on the field, almost dead,
With the blood through his sunny hair rippling
  From a horrible gash in the head.
They say he was first in the action,
  Gay-hearted, quick-handed, and witty;
He fought, till he fell with exhaustion,
  At the gates of our fair Southern city.

Fought and fell 'neath the guns of that city,
  With a spirit transcending his years.
Lift him up, in your large-hearted pity,
  And wet his pale lips with your tears.

Touch him gently—most sacred the duty
  Of dressing that poor shattered hand!
God spare him to rise in his beauty,
  And battle once more for his land!

Who groaned? What a passionate murmur—
  "*In Thy mercy, O God! let me die!*"
Ha! surgeon, your hand must be firmer;
  That grapeshot has shattered his thigh.
Fling the light on those poor furrowed features;
  Gray-haired and unknown, bless the brother!
O God! that one of Thy creatures
  Should e'er work such woe on another!

Wipe the sweat from his brow with your kerchief;
  Let the stained, tattered collar go wide.
See! he stretches out blindly to search if
  The surgeon still stands at his side.
"*My son's over yonder! he's wounded—
  Oh! this ball that's broken my thigh!*"
And again he burst out, all a-tremble,
  "*In Thy mercy, O God! let me die!*"

Pass on! It is useless to linger
  While others are claiming your care;

There's need of your delicate finger,
   For your womanly sympathy, there.
There are sick ones, athirst for caressing—
   There are dying ones, raving of home—
There are wounds to be bound with a blessing—
   And shrouds to make ready for some.

They have gathered about you the harvest
   Of death, in its ghastliest view;
The nearest, as well as the farthest,
   Is here with the traitor and true!
And crowned with your beautiful patience,
   Made sunny, with love at the heart,
You must balsam the wounds of a nation,
   Nor falter, nor shrink from your part!

Up and down, through the wards, where the fever
   Stalks noisome, and gaunt, and impure,
You must go, with your steadfast endeavor,
   To comfort, to counsel, to cure!
I grant that the task's superhuman,
   But strength will be given to you
To do for these dear ones what woman
   Alone in her pity can do.

And the lips of the mothers will bless you
As angels, sweet-visaged and pale!
And the little ones run to caress you,
While the wives and sisters cry *"Hail!"*
But e'en if you drop down unheeded,
What matter? God's ways are the best!
You have poured out your life where 'twas needed,
And He will take care of the rest!

The Burial of Latané.[11.]

THE combat raged not long, but ours the day;
  And, through the hosts that compassed us around,
Our little band rode proudly on its way,
  Leaving one gallant comrade, glory-crowned,
    Unburied on the field he died to gain—
    Single of all his men, amid the hostile slain.

One moment on the battle's edge he stood—
  Hope's halo, like a helmet, round his hair—
The next beheld him, dabbled in his blood,
  Prostrate in death; and yet, in death how fair!
    Even thus he passed through the red gates
      of strife,
    From earthly crowns and palms, to an immor-
      tal life.

A brother bore his body from the field,
  And gave it unto strangers' hands, that closed
The calm blue eyes, on earth forever sealed,
  And tenderly the slender limbs composed:
    Strangers, yet sisters, who, with Mary's love,
    Sat by the open tomb, and weeping, looked
      above.

little child strewed roses on his bier—
Pale roses, not more stainless than his soul,
or yet more fragrant than his life sincere,
That blossomed with good actions — brief, but
whole;
The aged matron and the faithful slave
Approached, with reverent feet, the hero's
lowly grave.

o man of God might say the burial rite
Above the "rebel"—thus declared the foe
iat blanched before him in the deadly fight;
But woman's voice, with accents soft and low,
Trembling with pity—touched with pathos—
read
Over his hallowed dust the ritual for the dead.

'*Tis sown in weakness, it is raised in power!*"
Softly the promise floated on the air,
hile the low breathings of the sunset hour
Came back responsive to the mourner's prayer.
Gently they laid him underneath the sod,
And left him with his fame, his country, and
his God!

Let us not weep for him, whose deeds endure!
  So young, so brave, so beautiful! He died
As he had wished to die; the past is sure;
  Whatever yet of sorrow may betide
     Those who still linger by the stormy shore,
     Change can not harm him now, nor fortur
       touch him more.

And when Virginia, leaning on her spear,
  Victrix et Vidua—the conflict done—
Shall raise her mailed hand to wipe the tear
  That starts, as she recalls each martyred son,
     No prouder memory her breast shall sway
     Than thine, our early lost, lamented Latané

The Guerrillas.

Awake and to horse! my brothers,
  For the dawn is glimmering gray,
And hark! in the crackling brushwood
  There are feet that tread this way!

"Who cometh?" "A friend!" "What tidings?"
  "O God! I sicken to tell;
For the earth seems earth no longer,
  And its sights are sights of hell!

"There's rapine, and fire, and slaughter,
  From the mountain down to the shore;
There's blood on the trampled harvest,
  And blood on the homestead floor!

"From the far off conquered cities
  Comes the voice of a stifled wail,
And the shrieks and moans of the houseless
  Ring out, like a dirge, on the gale!

"I've seen, from the smoking village
  Our mothers and daughters fly!

I've seen, where the little children
    Sank down in the furrows, to die!

" On the banks of the battle-stained river
    I stood, as the moonlight shone,
And it glared on the face of my brother,
    As the sad wave swept him on!

" Where my home was glad, are ashes,
    And horror and shame had been there;
For I found, on the fallen lintel,
    This tress of my wife's torn hair!

" They are turning the slave upon us,
    And with more than the fiend's worst art,
Have uncovered the fires of the savage,
    That slept in his untaught heart!

" The ties to our hearths that bound him,
    They have rent, with curses, away,
And maddened him, with their madness,
    To be almost as brutal as they.

" With halter, and torch, and Bible,
    And hymns, to the sound of the drum,

They preach the gospel of murder,
    And pray for lust's kingdom to come!

"To saddle! to saddle! my brothers!
    Look up to the rising sun,
And ask of the God who shines there,
    Whether deeds like these shall be done.

"Wherever the vandal cometh,
    Press home to his heart with your steel;
And where'er at his bosom ye can not,
    Like the serpent, go strike at his heel.

"Through thicket and wood go hunt him;
    Creep up to his camp-fire side!
And let ten of his corpses blacken
    Where one of our brothers hath died!

"In his fainting, foot-sore marches,
    In his flight from the stricken fray,
In the snare of the lonely ambush,
    The debts that we owe him, pay!

"In God's hand alone is judgment,
    But He strikes with the hands of men,

And His blight would wither our manhood,
  If we smote not the smiter again.

" By the graves where our fathers slumber,
    By the shrines where our mothers prayed,
  By our homes, and hopes, and freedom,
    Let every man swear on his blade—

" That he will not sheath nor stay it
    Till from point to heft it glow,
  With the flush of Almighty vengeance,
    In the blood of the felon foe !"

They swore ; and the answering sunlight
  Leapt red from their lifted swords,
And the hate in their hearts made echo
  To the wrath in their burning words !

There's weeping in all New-England,
  And by Schuylkill's bank a knell ;
And the widows there, and the orphans,
  How the oath was kept can tell.

The Lone Sentry.(III.)

'Twas as the dying of the day,
  The darkness grew so still;
The drowsy pipe of evening birds
  Was hushed upon the hill.
Athwart the shadows of the vale
  Slumbered the men of might;
And one lone sentry paced his rounds
  To watch the camp that night.

A grave and solemn man was he,
  With deep and sombre brow;
The dreamful eyes seemed hoarding up
  Some unaccomplished vow.
The wistful glance peered o'er the plain,
  Beneath the starry light;
And, with the murmured name of God,
  He watched the camp that night.

The future opened unto him
  Its grand and awful scroll—
Manassas and the valley march
  Came heaving o'er his soul;

Richmond and Sharpsburgh thundered by,
    With that tremendous fight
That gave him to the angel host,
    Who watched the camp that night.

We mourn for him, who died for us,
    With one resistless moan,
While up the Valley of the Lord
    He marches to the Throne!
He kept the faith of men and saints
    Sublime, and pure, and bright;
He sleeps—and all is well with him
    Who watched the camp that night.

Brothers! the midnight of the cause
    Is shrouded in our fate—
The demon Goths pollute our halls
    With fire, and lust, and hate!
Be strong—be valiant—be assured—
    Strike home for Heaven and Right!
The soul of Jackson stalks abroad,
    And guards the camp to-night!

Jackson.

Nor 'mid the lightning of the stormy fight,
Not in the rush upon the vandal foe,
Did kingly Death, with his resistless might,
　　Lay the Great Leader low.

His warrior soul its earthly shackles broke
In the full sunshine of a peaceful town.
When all the storm was hushed, the trusty oak
　　That propped our cause went down.

Though his alone the blood that flecks the ground,
Recording all his grand, heroic deeds,
Freedom herself is writhing with the wound,
　　And all the country bleeds.

He entered not the Nation's Promised Land,
At the red belching of the cannon's mouth;
But broke the House of Bondage with his hand—
　　The Moses of the South!

O gracious God! not gainless is the loss:
A glorious sunbeam gilds thy sternest frown;
And, while his country staggers with the Cross,
　　He rises with the Crown!

To the Exchanged Prisoners.

THE anchors are weighed, and the gates of your
    prison
  Fall wide, as your ship gives her prow to the
    foam,
And a few hurried hours shall return you exulting,
  Where the flag you have fought for floats over
    your home.

God send that not long may its folds be uplifted
  O'er fields dark and sad with the trail of the
    fight—
God give it the triumph He always hath given,
  Or sooner or later, to Valor and Right!

But if peace may not yet wreath your homes with
    her olive,
  And new victims are still round the altar to
    bleed,
God shield you amid the red bolts of the battle!
  God give you stout hearts for high thought and
    brave deed!

No need we should bid you go strike for your
    freedom—
You have stricken, like men, for its blessings
    before,
And your homes and your loved ones, your wrongs
    and your manhood,
Will nerve you to fight the good fight o'er and
    o'er !

But will you not think, as you wave your glad ban-
    ners,
How the flag of old Maryland, trodden in shame,
Lies sullied and torn in the dust of her highways—
And will you not strike a fresh blow in her name?

Her mothers have sent their first-born to be with
    you,
Wherever with blood there are fields to be won—
Her daughters have wept for you, clad you and
    nursed you—
Their vows and their hopes and their smiles are
    your own.

Let her cause be your cause, and whenever the
    war-cry
Bids you rush to the field, oh ! remember her too—

And when freedom and peace shall be blended in
     glory,
  Oh! count it your shame if she be not with you.

And if in the hour when pride, honor, and duty,
  Shall stir every throb in the hearts of brave men,
The wrongs of the helpless can quicken such pulses,
  Let the captives at Warren give flame to them
     then.

The Hero without a Name.

I LOVED, when a child, to seek the page
  Where war's proud tales are grandly told,
And to read of the might of that former age,
  In the brave, good days of old;
When men for Virtue and Honor fought
  In serried ranks, 'neath their banners bright,
By the fairy hands of beauty wrought,
  And broidered with " *God and Right.*"

'Twas there I read of Sir Launcelot true,
  Whose deeds have been sung in a nobler strain;
And of Roderic, the Bold, who his falchion drew,
  In the cause of his native Spain;
And, in thought, I beheld gay Sidney ride—
  His white plume dotting the field's expanse;
And Bayard, who came like the swirl of the tide,
  As he struck for the lilies of France.

On the crags of Scotland then I saw,
  With his hair of golden hue, Montrose;
And the swarthy Douglas, whose name was law
  In the homes of his English foes.

There was Winkelried, in the Swiss-land famed;
    And the mountaineers' boast—devoted Tell—
·Before whose patriot shaft, well-aimed,
    His country's tyrant fell.

'Neath Erin's flag, with its glad sunburst,
    Was Emmett, the first in that martyr van,
Whose blood makes sacred the gibbet accursed,
    Where they died for the rights of man.
There was Light-Horse Harry, the first in the fray,
    There was Marion leading his cavaliers—
And Washington, too, whose grave to-day,
    Is the shrine of patriot tears.

These splendid forms were part of the throng
    That delighted me, moving in pageant grand,
Through the wastes of time and the fields of song,
    From the legends of every land.
But little I hoped myself to see
    A spirit akin to these stately men;
Or dreamed that great hearts, like theirs, could be
    In a prison's crowded pen.

Yet, I've seen in the wards of the hospital there,
    A hero, I fancy, as peerless of soul;

A pale-faced boy, whose home is fair,
　Where the waters of Cumberland roll.
On his narrow cot, in that narrow room,
　Where the music he hears is the sigh and the
　　groan,
He lies through the day's long pain and gloom,
　But he never makes a moan!

They hewed him down with their blades of steel,
　Where the troopers charged from the camp of the
　　foe;
But he was not killed—although I feel,
　It would have been better so;
For my heart within me is very sad,
　As I sit and hold his wasted hand,
And hear him tell of the days that were glad,
　In our own dear, sunny land.

There are hours, again, in his fever's heat,
　When his restless fancies fly to his home:
And he talks of the scythe in the falling wheat,
　And the reapers that go and come;
Of his boyish mates, in their frolicsome glee,
　In the cedarn glades and the woodlawns dim;
And how he carved there on many a tree,
　A name that was dear to him;

Of the sweet wild roses that scatter the light,
  Through the open door and the window-pane;
And October's haze, on the far off height—
  And the quiet country lane;
Of the rivulet's plash, and the song of birds,
  And the corn rows, standing like men with spears;
Of his mother's tones, and her loving words—
  And his cheeks are wet with tears.

And I seem to see her, as autumn leaves
  Like shadows fall in the lonely glen,
And the swallows come home to those silent eaves,
  Where *he* shall not come again.
And then I rejoice that she can not see,
  How the blight has stained her fairest bloom;
I am glad her footstep will never be
  Beside his northern tomb.

And I think of another, who watches too,
  When the early stars are bright on the hill,
Nor dreams that his heart—so confiding and true—
  Will soon be forever still.
Ah! many, in vain, to their hopes shall cling,
  Through the dreary morn and the mournful eve;
And memory alone shall its solace bring,
  To a thousand hearts that grieve.

My comrade will last but a little while;
   For I see on every succeeding day,
A fainter flush—but a sweeter smile—
   Over his features play.
And he knows that until he is under the sod,
   These walls, little better, shall shut him in;
But his soul puts trust in the Lamb of God,
   That taketh away all sin!

And somehow I think, when our lives are done,
   That this humble hero—without a name—
Will be greater up there, than many a one
   Of the high-born men of fame.
And I know I would rather wear to-day,
   The crown that is his, with its fadeless bloom,
Than Roderic's helm, so golden and gay,
   Or Sidney's snow-white plume!

O prisoner boy! that I were as near,
   As you are now to that "shining shore,"
Where the waters of life and of love are clear,
   And weeping shall come no more.
It can not be now; yet, in God's own time,
   When He calls his weary ones home to rest,
May I join with you in the angel chime—
   Like you, be a welcome guest!

The Cavalier's Glee.

Spur on! spur on! we love the bounding
Of barbs, that bear us to the fray :
" *The charge*" our bugles now are sounding
And our bold Stuart leads the way!
The path to honor lies before us;
Our hated foemen gather fast!
At home, bright eyes are sparkling for us,
And we'll defend them to the last!

Spur on! spur on! we love the rushing
Of steeds that spurn the turf they tread;
We'll through the northern ranks go crushing,
With our proud banner overhead!
The path to honor lies before us,
Our hated foemen gather fast!
At home, bright eyes are sparkling for us,
And we'll defend them to the last!

Spur on! spur on! we love the flashing
Of blades that battle for the free !
'Tis for our sunny south they're clashing—
For household gods and liberty !

The path to honor lies before us ;
Our hated foemen gather fast !
At home, bright eyes are sparkling for us,
And we'll defend them to the last !

The River.

THEY slept on the field that their valor had won!
But arose with the first, early blush of the sun,
For they knew that a great deed remained to be
      done,
    When they passed o'er the river.

They rose with the sun, caught new life from his
      light—
Those giants of courage, those Anaks in fight—
And they laughed out aloud in the joy of their
      might,
    Marching swift for the River.

On! on! like the rushing of storms through the
      hills—
On! on! with a tramp that is firm as their wills—
And the one heart of thousands grows buoyant
      and thrills,
    At the thought of the River.

On! the sheen of their swords! the fierce gleam of
    their eyes!
It seemed as on earth a new sunlight would rise,
And king-like, flash up to the sun in the skies,
       O'er the path to the River.

But their banners, shot-scarred, and all darkened
    with gore—
On a strong wind of morn streaming wildly before—
Like the wings of Death-angels, swept fast to the
    shore,
       The green shore of the River.

As they march—from the hill-side, the hamlet, the
    stream—
Gaunt throngs, whom the foeman had manacled,
    teem,
Like men just aroused from some terrible dream,
       To pass o'er the River.

They behold the broad banners, blood-darkened,
    yet fair,
And a moment dissolves the last spell of despair,
While a peal, as of victory, swells on the air,
       Rolling out to the River.

And that cry, with a thousand strange echoings
      spread,
Till the ashes of heroes seemed stirred in their bed,
And the deep voice of passion surged up from the
      dead—
      Ay! press on to the River.

On! on! like the rushing of storms through the
      hills—
On! on! with a tramp that is firm as their wills,
And the one heart of thousands grows buoyant
      and thrills
      As they pause by the River.

Then the wan face of Maryland—haggard and worn—
At that sight, lost the touch of its aspect forlorn,
As she turned on her foemen, full statured in scorn,
      Pointing stern to the River.

And Potomac flowed calm, scarcely heaving her
      breast,
With her low-lying billows kissed warm by the
      west;
For the hand of the Lord lulled the waters to rest
      Of the far rolling River.

Passed! passed! the glad thousands march safe
    through the tide—
(Hark, despots! and hear the wild knell of your
    pride
Ringing weird-like and wild—pealing up from the
    side
    Of the calm flowing River.)

'Neath a blow swift and mighty, the tyrant shall
    fall!
Vain! vain! to his God swells the desolate call!
For his grave has been hollowed and woven his
    pall,
    As they passed o'er the River.

A Poem that needs no Dedication. [IV.]

WHAT! ye hold yourselves as freemen?
　　Tyrants love just such as ye!
Go! abate your lofty manner!
Write upon the State's old banner,
　　　　"*A furore Normanorum,*
　　　　Libera nos, O Domine!"

Sink before the Federal altar,
　　Each one, low on bended knee;
Pray, with lips that sob and falter,
This prayer from a coward's Psalter:
　　　　"*A furore Normanorum,*
　　　　Libera nos, O Domine!"

But ye hold that quick repentance
　　In the Northern mind will be;
This repentance comes no sooner
Than the robber's did, at Luna.
　　　　"*A furore Normanorum,*
　　　　Libera nos, O Domine!"

He repented him; the Bishop
  Gave him absolution free—
Poured upon him sacred chrism
In the pomp of his baptism.
      "A furore Normanorum,
      Libera nos, O Domine!"

He repented; then he sickened
  Was he pining for the sea?
In extremis he was shriven.
The viaticum was given:
      " A furore Normanorum,
      Libera nos, O Domine!"

Then the old cathedral's choir
  Took the plaintive minor key,
With the host upraised before him,
Down the marble aisle they bore him:
      " A furore Normanorum,
      Libera nos, O Domine!"

While the Bishop and the Abbot,
  All the monks of high degree—
Chanting praise to the Madonna,
Came to do him Christian honor.
      " A furore Normanorum,
      Libera nos. O Domine!"

Now the *Miserere's* cadence
  Takes the voices of the sea;
As the music-billows quiver
See the dead freebooter shiver!
      "*A furore Normanorum,*
      Libera nos, O Domine!"

Is it that those intonations
  Thrill him thus, from head to knee?
Lo! his cerements burst asunder!
'Tis a sight of fear and wonder!
      "*A furore Normanorum,*
      Libera nos, O Domine!"

Fierce he stands before the Bishop—
  Dark as shape of Destinie!
Hark! a shriek ascends appalling!
Down the prelate goes—dead—falling!
      "*A furore Normanorum,*
      Libera nos, O Domine!"

HASTING lives! he was but feigning!
  What! Repentant? Never he!
Down he smites the priests and friars,
And the city lights with fires.
      "*A furore Normanorum,*
      Libera nos, O Domine!"

Ah! the children and the maidens,
 'Tis in vain they strive to flee!
Where the white-haired priests lie bleeding
Is no place for tearful pleading,
  "A furore Normanorum,
  Libera nos, O Domine!"

Louder swells the frightful tumult—
 Pallid death holds revelrie!
Dies the organ's mighty clamor
By the Norseman's iron hammer!
  "A furore Normanorum,
  Libera nos, O Domine!"

So they thought that he'd repented!
 Had they nailed him to a tree,
He had not deserved their pity,
And they——had not lost their city.
  "A furore Normanorum,
  Libera nos, O Domine!"

For the moral in this story,
 Which is plain as truth can be:
If we trust the North's relenting,
We will shriek, too late repenting,
  "A furore Normanorum,
  Libera nos, O Domine!"

Dirge for Ashby.

HEARD ye that thrilling word—
  Accent of dread!
Fall like a thunderbolt,
  Bowing each head?
Over the battle dun—
Over each booming gun—
    Ashby, our bravest one!
    Ashby is dead!

Saw ye the veterans—
  Hearts that had known
Never a quail of fear,
  Never a groan—
Sob 'mid the fight they win,
Tears their stern eyes within?
    Ashby, our paladin!
    Ashby is dead!

Dash, dash the tear away!
  Crush down the pain!
Dulce et decus be
  Fittest refrain.

Why should the dreary pall
Round him be flung at all?
Did not our hero fall,
     Gallantly slain?

Catch the last words of cheer
    Dropped from his tongue!
Over the volley's din
    Let them be rung!
"*Follow me! Follow me!*"
Soldier! oh! could there be
Pæan, or dirge for thee
    Loftier sung?

Bold as the Lion's Heart—
    Dauntless and brave;
Knightly as knightliest
    Bayard could crave;
Sweet—with all Sidney's grace—
Tender as Hampden's face—
Who, who shall fill the space,
    Void by his grave?

'T is not one broken heart,
    Wild with dismay—

Crazed in her agony—
　　Weeps o'er his clay!
Ah! from a thousand eyes
Flow the pure tears that rise—
Widowed VIRGINIA lies
　　　　Stricken to-day!

Yet, charge as gallantly,
　　Ye whom he led!
Jackson, the victor, still
　　Stands at your head!
Heroes! be battle done,
Bravelier every one,
Nerved by the thought alone—
　　　Ashby is dead!

A Ballad for the Young South.

MEN of the South! Our foes are up
    In fierce and grim array;
Their sable banner laps the air—
    An insult to the day!
The saints of Cromwell rise again,
    In sanctimonious hordes,
Hiding behind the garb of peace
    A million ruthless swords.
From North, and East, and West, they seek
    The same disastrous goal,
With CHRIST upon the lying lip,
    And Satan in the soul!
Mocking, with ancient shibboleth,
    All wise and just restraints:
"*To saints of Heaven was empire given,*
    And WE, alone, are saints!"

A preacher to the pulpit comes
    And calls upon the crowd,
For Southern creeds and Southern hopes
    To weave a bloody shroud.

Beside the prayer-book, on his desk,
    The bullet-mould is seen;
And near the Bible's golden clasp,
    The dagger's stately sheen;
The simple tale of Bethlehem
    No more is fondly told,
For every priestly surplice drags
    Too heavily with gold;
The blessed Cross of Calvary
    Becomes a sign of Baal,
Like that which played when chieftains raised
    The clansmen of the Gael!

Hark to the howling demagogues—
    A fierce and ravenous pack—
With nostrils prone, and bark, and bay,
    That close upon our track:
"Down with the laws our fathers made!
    They bind our hearts no more;
Down with the stately edifice,
    Cemented with their gore!
Forget the legends of our race—
    Efface each wise decree—
Americans must kneel as slaves,
    Till Africans are free!

Out on the mere Caucasian blood
  Of Teuton, Celt, or Gaul!
The stream that springs from Niger's source
  Must triumph over all!"

So speaks a solemn senator
  Within those halls to-day,
That echoed erst, the thunder-burst
  Of WEBSTER and of CLAY!
Look North, look East, look West—the scene
  Is blackening all around;
The negro cordon, year by year,
  Is fast and faster bound;
The black line crossed—the sable flag
  Surrounded by a host—
Our out-post forced, our sentinels
  Asleep upon their posts;
Our brethren's life-blood flowing free,
  To stain the Kansas soil—
And shed in vain, while pious thieves
  Are fattening on our toil!
Look North—look West—the ominous sky
  Is starless, moonless, black,
And from the East comes hurrying up
  A sweeping thunder-rack!

Men of the South! Ye have no kin
  With fanatics, or fools;
Ye are not bound by breed, or birth,
  To Massachusetts rules!
A hundred nations gave their blood
  To feed these healthful springs,
Which bear the seed of *Jacques Bonhomme,*
  With those of Bourbon kings.
The Danish pluck and sailor craft—
  The Huguenotic will—
The Norman grace and chivalry—
  The German steady skill—
The fiery Celt's impassioned thought
  Inspire the Southron's heart,
Which has no room for bigot-gloom,
  Or pious plunder's art!

Sons of the brave! The time has come
  To bow the haughty crest,
Or stand alone, despite the threats
  Of North, or East, or West!
The hour has come for manly deeds
  And not for puling words;
The place is passed for platform prate—
  It is the time for swords!

Now, by the fame of JOHN CALHOUN,
  To honest truth be true!
And by old JACKSON's iron will,
  Now do what ye can do!
By all ye love—by all ye hope—
  Be resolute and proud;
And make your flag a symbol high
  Of triumph, or a shroud!

Men of the South! Look up—behold
  The deep and sullen gloom,
That darkles o'er our sunny land
  With thunder in its womb!
Are ye so blind ye can not see
  The omens in the sky?
Are ye so deaf ye can not hear
  The tramp of foemen nigh?
Are ye so dull ye will endure
  The whips and scorn of men,
Who wear the heart of TITUS OATES
  Beneath the face of PENN?
Never, I ween! and foot to foot,
  Ye now will gladly stand
For land and life, for child and wife,
  With naked steel in hand!

Ashby.

To the brave all homage render!
    Weep, ye skies of June!
With a radiance pure and tender,
    Shine, oh, saddened moon!
"*Dead upon the field of glory!*"—
Hero fit for song and story—
    Lies our bold dragoon!

Well they learned, whose hands have slain him,
    Braver, knightlier foe,
Never fought 'gainst Moor or Paynim—
    Rode at Templestowe:
With a mien how high and joyous,
'Gainst the hordes that would destroy us
    Went he forth, we know.

Never more, alas! shall sabre
    Gleam around his crest—
Fought his fight, fulfilled his labor,
    Stilled his manly breast—
All unheard sweet nature's cadence,
Trump of fame and voice of maidens,
    Now he takes his rest.

Earth, that all too soon hath bound him,
  Gently wrap his clay!
Linger lovingly around him,
  Light of dying day!
Softly fall, ye summer showers—
Birds and bees, among the flowers
  Make the gloom seem gay!

Then, throughout the coming ages,
  When his sword is rust,
And his deeds in classic pages—
  Mindful of her trust—
Shall VIRGINIA, bending lowly,
Still a ceaseless vigil holy
  Keep, above his dust!

___

There's Life in the Old Land yet. [v.]

By blue Patapsco's billowy dash,
  The tyrant's war-shout comes,
Along with the cymbal's fitful clash,
  And the growl of his sullen drums.
We hear it! we heed it, with vengeful thrills,
  And we shall not forgive or forget—
There's faith in the streams, there's hope in the
       hills—
"There's life in the Old Land yet!"

Minions! we sleep, but we are not dead;
  We are crushed, we are scourged, we are scarred;
We crouch—'tis to welcome the triumph-tread
  Of the peerless Beauregard!
Then woe to your vile, polluting horde,
  When the Southern braves are met;
There's faith in the victor's stainless sword—
"There's life in the Old Land yet!"

Bigots! ye quell not the valiant mind,
  With the clank of an iron chain;

The Spirit of Freedom sings in the wind,
  O'er Merryman, Thomas, and Kane!
And we, though we smite not, are not thralls—
  We are piling a gory debt;
E'en down by McHenry's dungeon walls,
  "There's life in the Old Land yet!"

Our women have hung their harps away,
  And they scowl on your brutal bands,
While the nimble poignard dares the day
  In their dear, defiant hands;
They will strip their tresses to string our bows,
  Ere the Northern sun is set;
There's faith in their unrelenting woes—
  "There's life in the Old Land yet!"

There's life though it throbbeth in silent veins;
  'Tis vocal, without noise;
It gushed o'er Manassas' solemn plains
  In the blood of the *Maryland boys!*
That blood shall cry aloud, and rise
  With an everlasting threat—
By the death of the brave!—by the God in the
    skies!—
  "There's life in the Old Land yet!"

A Cry to Arms.

Ho ! woodsmen of the mountain side !
  Ho ! dwellers in the vales !
Ho ! ye, that by the chafing tide
  Have roughened in the gales !
Leave barn and byre, leave kin and cot,
  Lay by the bloodless spade ;
Let desk, and case, and counter rot,
  And burn your books of trade !

The despot roves your fairest lands,
  And till he flies, or fears,
·Your fields must grow but armèd bands—
  Your sheaves be sheaves of spears !
Give up to mildew and to rust
  The useless tools of gain ;
And feed your country's sacred dust
  With floods of crimson rain !

Come with the weapons at your call—
  With musket, pike, or knife ;
He wields the deadliest blade of all
  Who lightest holds his life.

The arm that drives its unbought blows
  With all a patriot's scorn,
Might brain a tyrant with a rose,
  Or stab him with a thorn!

Does any falter? let him turn
  To some brave maiden's eyes,
And catch the holy fires that burn
  In those sublunar skies.
Oh! could you like your women feel
  And in their spirit march,
A day might see your lines of steel
  Beneath the victor's arch!

What hope, O God! would not grow warm
  When thoughts like these give cheer?
The lily calmly braves the storm—
  And shall the palm-tree fear?
No! rather let its branches court
  The rack that sweeps the plain;
And from the lily's regal port
  Learn how to breast the strain.

Ho! woodsmen of the mountain side
  Ho! dwellers in the vales!

Ho! ye, that by the roaring tide,
Have roughened in the gales!
Come! flocking gayly to the fight,
From forest, hill, and lake!
We battle for our country's right
And for the lily's sake!

The Barefooted Boys.

.

By the sword of St. Michael
  The old dragon through!
By David his sling,
  And the giant he slew!
Let us write us a rhyme,
  As a record to tell,
How the South on a time
  Stormed the ramparts of hell
        With her barefooted boys!

Had the South in her border
  A hero to spare,
Or a heart at her altar,
  Lo! its life's blood was there!
And the black battle-grime
  Might never disguise
The smile of the South,
  On the lips and the eyes
        Of her barefooted boys!

There's a grandeur in fight,
  And a terror the while,

But none like the light
　Of that terrible smile—
The smile of the South,
　When the storm-cloud unrolls
The lightning that loosens
　The wrath in the souls
　　　Of her barefooted boys!

It withered the foe
　Like the red light that runs
Through the dead forest leaves,
　And he fled from his guns!
Grew the smile to a laugh,
　Rose the laugh to a yell,
As the iron-clad hoofs
　Clattered back into hell
　　　From our barefooted boys.

The Tennessee Exile's Song.

I HEAR the rushing of her streams,
  The murmuring of her trees,
The exile's anguish swells my heart
  And melts with each soft breeze.
'Midst other scenes her corn-hills wave,
  Her mountains pierce the sky—
Where, where are they who swore to save—
  To conquer, or to die?

They come, from every blue hill-side,
  From every lovely dale,
The heart, the soul, the very pride
  Of mountain, hill, and vale.
Stalwart, they court like Anak's sons,
  The rapture of the strife;
Drink in the earthquake of the guns,
  To them the breath of life.

Spare not the invading mongrel hordes,
  But slay them as they stand!
Strike! Tennessee has living swords,
  The best in all the land!

Strew o'er her plains their hostile lines,
  Drench her fair fields with blood,
Fill their long ranks with bitter groans—
  Let blood flow like a flood!

Ay, sow the seeds of lasting hate
  At Johnson's, Hatlin's graves,
And do their deeds and dare their fate,
  Or live the oppressors' slaves!
Bleed freely, as you bled of yore,
  In every well-fought field,
Press round the flag you always bore
  The foremost—as a shield

  .   .   .   .

I feel her pulse beat high and quick,
  Her sinews stretch for strife,
Full come her heart-throbs deep and thick,
  She kindles into life!
Though Donelson has told her tale,
  And Shiloh's page is bright,
There's yet a bloodier field to win,
  For Nashville and the right!

Somebody's Darling.

Into a ward of the whitewashed walls
    Where the dead and the dying lay—
Wounded by bayonets, shells and balls—
    Somebody's darling was borne one day.
Somebody's darling! so young and so brave,
    Wearing still on his pale, sweet face—
Soon to be hid by the dust of the grave—
    The lingering light of his boyhood's grace.

Matted and damp are the curls of gold,
    Kissing the snow of that fair young brow;
Pale are the lips of delicate mould—
    Somebody's darling is dying now.
Back from the beautiful, blue-veined face
    Brush every wandering, silken thread;
Cross his hands as a sign of grace—
    Somebody's darling is still and dead!

Kiss him once for *somebody's* sake;
    Murmur a prayer, soft and low;
One bright curl from the cluster take—
    They were somebody's pride, you know.

Somebody's hand hath rested there;
  Was it a mother's, soft and white?
And have the lips of a sister fair
  Been baptized in those waves of light?

God knows best. He was somebody's love;
  Somebody's heart enshrined him here;
Somebody wafted his name above,
  Night and morn, on the wings of prayer.
Somebody wept when he marched away,
  Looking so handsome, brave and grand;
Somebody's kiss on his forehead lay;
  Somebody clung to his parting hand—

Somebody's watching and waiting for him,
  Yearning to hold him again to her heart:
There he lies—with the blue eyes dim,
  And smiling, child-like lips apart.
Tenderly bury the fair young dead,
  Pausing to drop on his grave a tear,
Carve on the wooden slab at his head,
  "*Somebody's darling lies buried here!*"

Monody on Jackson.

Ay, toll! toll! toll!
  Toll the funeral bell!
So let its mournful echoes roll
From sphere to sphere, from pole to pole,
O'er the flight of the greatest, kingliest soul
  That ever in battle fell.

Yes, weep! weep! weep!
  Weep for the hero fled!
For Death, the greatest of soldiers, at last
Has o'er our leader his black pall cast.
From earth his noble form hath passed
  To the home of the mighty dead.

Then toll! and weep! and mourn!
  Mourn the fall of the brave!
For Jackson, whose deeds made the nation
    proud,
Whose very name was a war-song loud,
With the "crimson cross" for his martial
    shroud—
  Now sleeps his long sleep in the grave.

His form has passed away—
　His voice is silent and still—
No more, at the head of "the old brigade"—
The daring men who were never dismayed—
Will he lead them to glory that never can fade
　STONEWALL, of the Iron Will!

He fell as a hero should fall;
　'Mid the thunder of war he died.
While the rifle cracked and the cannon roared,
And the blood of the friend and foeman poured,
He dropped from his nerveless grasp the sword
　That erst was the nation's pride.

Virginia, his mother, is bowed;
　Her eyelids heavy and low.
From all the South comes the wailing moan,
And mountain and valley reëcho the groan,
For the gallant chief of her clans has flown—
　The nation is filled with woe.

Rest, warrior! rest!
　Rest in thy laureled tomb!
Thy mem'ry shall live to earth's latest years,
Thy name shall still raise the despot's fears,
While over thee falls a nation's tears;
　Thy deeds shall not perish in gloom!

Coercion:

A POEM FOR THEN AND NOW.

Who talks of Coercion? who dares to deny
  A resolute people the right to be free?
Let him blot out forever one star from the sky,
  Or curb with his fetter the wave of the sea!

Who prates of Coercion? can love be restored
  To bosoms where only resentment may dwell?
Can peace on earth be proclaimed by the sword,
  Or good-will among men be established by shell?

Shame! shame!—that the statesman and trickster,
      forsooth,
  Should have for a crisis no other recourse,
Beneath the fair day-spring of light and of truth,
  Than the old *brutum fulmen* of tyranny,—force!

From the holes where Fraud, Falsehood, and Hate
    slink away;
  From the crypt in which Error lies buried in
    chains;

This foul apparition stalks forth to the day,
  And would ravage the land which his presence
    profanes.

Could you conquer us, Men of the North—could you
    bring
  Desolation and death on our homes as a flood—
Can you hope the pure lily, Affection, will spring
  From ashes all reeking and sodden with blood?

Could you brand us as villains and serfs, know ye
    not
  What fierce, sullen hatred lurks under the scar?
How loyal to Hapsburg is Venice, I wot!
  How dearly the Pole loves his Father, the Czar!

But 'twere well to remember this land of the sun
  Is a *nutrix leonum*, and suckles a race
Strong-armed, lion-hearted, and banded as one,
  Who brook not oppression and know not disgrace.

And well may the schemers in office beware
  The swift retribution that waits upon crime,
When the lion, RESISTANCE, shall leap from his lair,
  With a fury that renders his vengeance sublime.

Once, Men of the North, we were brothers, and
    still,
Though brothers no more, we would gladly be
    friends;
Nor join in a conflict accursed, that must fill
    With ruin the country on which it descends.

But, if smitten with blindness, and mad with the rage
    The gods gave to all whom they wished to des-
    troy,
You would act a new Iliad, to darken the age
    With horrors beyond what is told us of Troy—

If, deaf as the adder itself to the cries,
    When Wisdom, Humanity, Justice implore,
You would have our proud eagle to feed on the eyes
    Of those who have taught him so grandly to soar—

If there be to your malice no limit imposed,
    And you purpose hereafter to rule with the rod
The men upon whom you have already closed
    Our goodly domain and the temples of God:

To the breeze then your banner dishonored unfold,
    And, at once, let the tocsin be sounded afar;

We greet you, as greeted the Swiss Charles, the
    Bold—
With a farewell to peace and a welcome to war!

For the courage that clings to our soil, ever bright,
    Shall catch inspiration from turf and from tide;
Our sons unappalled shall go forth to the fight,
    With the smile of the fair, the pure kiss of the
        bride;

And the bugle its echoes shall send through the
    past,
In the trenches of Yorktown to waken the slain;
While the sod of King's Mountain shall heave at
    the blast,
    And give up its heroes to glory again.

The War-Christian's Thanksgiving. (vi.)

RESPECTFULLY DEDICATED TO THE WAR-CLERGY OF THE UNITED
STATES, BISHOPS, PRIESTS, AND DEACONS.

Cursed be he that doeth the work of the Lord negligently, and cursed be he that
epeth back his sword from blood.—*Jeremiah* 48 : 10.

O GOD of Battles! once again,
   With banner, trump, and drum,
And garments in Thy wine-press dyed,
   To give Thee thanks, we come!

No goats or bullocks, garlanded,
   Unto thine altars go—
With brothers' blood, by brothers shed,
   Our glad libations flow.

From pest-house and from dungeon foul
   Where, maimed and torn, they die;
From gory trench and charnel-house,
   Where, heap on heap, they lie:

In every groan that yields a soul,
   Each shriek a heart that rends—

With every breath of tainted air—
Our homage, Lord, ascends.

We thank thee for the sabre's gash,
The cannon's havoc wild;
We bless Thee for the widow's tears,
The want that starves her child.

We give Thee praise, that Thou hast lit
The torch and fanned the flame;
That lust and rapine hunt their prey,
Kind Father! in Thy name;

That, for the songs of idle joy
False angels sang of yore,
Thou sendest War on Earth, Ill Will
To Men, for evermore.

We know that wisdom, truth, and right
To us and ours are given—
That thou hast clothed us with the wrath
To do the work of Heaven.

We know that plains and cities waste
Are pleasant in Thine eyes;

Thou lov'st a hearthstone desolate,
  Thou lov'st a mourner's cries.

Let not our weakness fall below
  The measure of Thy will,
And while the press hath wine to bleed,
  Oh! tread it with us still!

Teach us to hate—as Jesus taught
  Fond fools, of yore, to love—
Grant us Thy vengeance as our own,
  Thy Pity, hide above.

Teach us to turn, with reeking hands,
  The pages of Thy word,
And hail the blessed curses there,
  On them that sheathe the sword.

Where'er we tread, may deserts spring,
  Till none are left to slay;
And when the last red drop is shed,
  We'll kneel again—and pray!

Virginians of the Valley.

SIC JURAT.

The knightliest of the knightly race,
   Who, since the days of old,
Have kept the lamp of chivalry
   Alight in hearts of gold—
The kindliest of the kindly band
   Who rarely hated ease,
Who rode with Smith around the land
   And Raleigh round the seas!

Who climbed the blue Virginia hills,
   Amid embattled foes,
And planted there, in valleys fair,
   The lily and the rose;
Whose fragrance lives in many lands,
   Whose beauty stars the earth,
And lights the hearths of many homes
   With loveliness and worth!

We thought they slept! these sons who kept
   The names of noble sires,

And slumbered, while the darkness crept
  Around their vigil fires!
But still the Golden Horse-shoe knights,
  Their Old Dominion keep,
Whose foes have found enchanted ground,
  But not a knight asleep!

The Ballad of the Right.

IN other days our fathers' love was loyal, full, and
    free,
For those they left behind them, on the Island of
    the Sea;
They fought the battles of King George and toasted
    him in song—
For then the Right kept proudly down the tyranny
    of Wrong.

But when the King's weak, willing slaves laid tax
    upon the tea,
The western men rose up and braved the Island of
    the Sea;
And swore a solemn oath to God, those men of
    iron might—
That at their hands the Wrong should die and up
    should go the Right!

The King sent over hireling hosts—Briton, Hessian,
    Scot—
And swore in turn those Western men, when cap-
    tured, should be shot;

While Chatham spoke with earnest tongue against
    the hireling throng,
And mournful saw the Right go down, and place
    give to the Wrong. .

But God was on the righteous side, and Gideon's
    sword was out,
With clash of steel, and rattling drum, and freeman's
    thunder-shout;
And crimson torrents drenched the land through that
    long, stormy fight,
But in the end, hurrah! the Wrong was beaten by
    the Right!

And when again the foemen came from out the
    Northern Sea,
To desolate our smiling land and subjugate the free,
Our fathers rushed to drive them back, with rifles
    keen and long,
And swore a mighty oath the Right should subju-
    gate the Wrong.

And while the world was looking on, the strife un-
    certain grew,
But soon aloft rose up our stars amid a field of blue;

For Jackson fought on red Chalmette, and won the
    glorious fight,
And then the Wrong went down, hurrah! and triumph
    crowned the Right!

The day has come again, when all who love the
    beauteous South,
Must speak, if needs be, for the Right, though by
    the cannon's mouth;
For foes accursed of God and man, with lying speech
    and song,
Would bind, imprison, hang the Right, and deify
    the Wrong.

But canting knave of pen and sword, or sanctimo-
    nious fool,
Shall never win this Southern land, to cripple, bind,
    and rule;
We'll muster on each bloody plain, thick as the stars
    of night,
And, through the help of God, the Wrong shall
    perish by the Right.

Zollicoffer.

FIRST in the fight, and first in the arms
    Of the white-winged angels of glory,
With the heart of the South at the feet of God,
    And his wounds to tell the story;

For the blood that flowed from his hero heart,
    On the spot where he nobly perished,
Was drunk by the earth as a sacrament
    In the holy cause he cherished!

In Heaven a home with the brave and blessed,
    And for his soul's sustaining
The apocalyptic eyes of Christ—
    And nothing on earth remaining,

But a handful of dust in the land of his choice,
    A name in song and story—
And fame to shout with immortal voice:
    DEAD ON THE FIELD OF GLORY!

A Word with the West. (vii.)

ONCE more to the breach for the Land of the West!
And a leader we give, of our bravest and best,
    Of his State and his army the pride;
Hope shines like the plume of Navarre on his crest,
    And gleams in the glaive at his side.

For his courage is keen and his honor is bright
As the trusty Toledo he wears to the fight,
    Newly wrought in the forges of Spain, (viii.)
And this weapon, like all he has brandished for Right,
    Will never be dimmed by a stain.

He leaves the loved soil of Virginia behind,
Where the dust of his fathers is fitly enshrined,
    Where lie the fresh fields of his fame;
Where the murmurous pines, (ix.) as they sway in the
      wind,
    Seem ever to whisper his name.

The Johnstons have always borne wings on their spurs,
And their motto a noble distinction confers,
    "*Ever Ready*"—for friend or for foe—

With a patriot's fervor the sentiment stirs
    The large, manly heart of our JOE.

We recall that a former bold chief of the clan
Fell, bravely defending the West, in the van,
    On Shiloh's illustrious day;
And with reason we reckon our Johnston the man
    The dark, bloody debt to repay.

There is much to be done: if not glory to seek,
There's a just and a terrible vengeance to wreak
    For crimes of a terrible dye,
While the plaint of the helpless, the wail of the weak
    In a chorus rise up to the sky.

For the Wolf of the North, we once drove to his
      den,
That quailed in affright 'neath the stern glance of
      men,
    With his pack has returned to the spoil;
Then come from the hamlet, the mountain, the glen,
    And drive him again from the soil!

Brave-born TENNESSEANS, so loyal, so true,
Who have hunted the beast in your highlands, of *you*
    Our leader has never a doubt;

You will troop by the thousand the chase to renew
  The day when his bugles ring out.

But ye "HUNTERS" so famed "OF KENTUCKY" of
    yore,
Where, where are the rifles that kept from your door
  The wolf and the robber as well?
Of a truth, you have never been laggard before
  To deal with a savage so fell.

Has the love you once bore to your country grown
    cold?
Has the fire on the altar died out? Do you hold
  Your lives than your freedom more dear?
Can you shamefully barter your birthright for gold,
  Or basely take counsel of fear?

We will not believe it—KENTUCKY, the land
Of a CLAY, will not tamely submit to the brand
  That disgraces the dastard, the slave;
The hour of redemption draws nigh—is at hand—
  Her own sons her own honor shall save!

Mighty men of MISSOURI, come forth to the call,
With the rush of your rivers when tempests appall,
  And the torrents their sources unseal;

And this be the watchword of one and of all—
"*Remember the butcher*, McNiel!"

Then once more to the breach for the land of the
West!
Strike home for your hearts—for the lips you love
best—
Follow on where your Leader you see!
One flash of his sword when the foe is hard pressed,
And the Land of the West shall be free!

You can Never Win them Back.

You can never win them back—
　　　　Never! never!
Though they perish on the track
　　　　Of your endeavor:
Though their corses strew the earth,
That smiled to give them birth;
And blood pollutes each hearth—
　　　　Ay, forever!

They have risen to a man,
　　　　Stern and fearless;
Of your boasting and your ban
　　　　They are careless;
Every hand has grasped its knife,
Every gun is primed for strife,
Every palm contains a life
　　　　High and peerless!

You have no such blood as theirs
　　　　For the shedding!
In the veins of cavaliers
　　　　Was its heading:

You have no such noble men
In your "abolition den,"
To march through foe and fen—
        Nothing dreading!

They may fall before the fire
        Of your legions,
Paid with gold for murderous hire—
        Bought allegiance!
But for every drop you shed
They will make a mound of dead,
That the vultures may be fed
        In our regions!

But the battle to the strong
        Is not given.
While the Judge of right and wrong
        Sits in heaven—
While the God of David still
Guides the pebble, with His will—
There are giants yet to kill—
        Wrongs unshriven!

Beauregard's Appeal. [x.]

YEA! though the need is bitter,
  Take down those sacred bells!
Whose music speaks of our hallowed joys
  And passionate farewells!

But ere ye fall dismantled,
  Ring out, deep Bells! once more:
And pour on the waves of the passing wind
  The symphonies of yore:

Let the latest born be welcomed
  By pealings glad and long;
Let the latest dead in the churchyard bed,
  Be laid with solemn song;

And the bells above them throbbing,
  Should sound in mournful tone,
As if in the grief for a human death,
  They prophesied their own.

Who says 'tis a desecration
  To strip the Temple Towers,
And invest the metal of peaceful notes
  With death-compelling powers?

A truce to cant and folly!
    With Faith itself at stake,
Shall we heed the cry of the shallow fool,
    Or pause for the Bigot's sake?

Then, crush the struggling sorrow!
    Feed high your furnace fires,
That shall mould into deep-mouthed guns of
        bronze,
    The Bells from a hundred spires.

Methinks no common vengeance—
    No transient war eclipse—
Will follow the awful thunder burst
    From their "adamantine lips."

A cause like ours is holy,
    And useth holy things;
And over the storm of a righteous strife,
    May shine the Angel's wings.

Where'er our duty leads us,
    The Grace of God is there,
And the lurid shrine of War may hold
    The Eucharist of prayer.

The Cameo Bracelet.

Eva sits on the ottoman there,
  Sits by a Psyche carved in stone,
With just such a face and just such an air
  As Esther upon her throne.

She's sifting lint for the brave who bled,
  And I watch her fingers float and flow
Over the linen, as thread by thread,
  It flakes to her lap like snow.

A bracelet clinks on her delicate wrist,
  Wrought as Cellini's were at Rome,
Out of the tears of the amethyst
  And the wan Vesuvian foam.

And full on the bauble-crest alway—
  A cameo image keen and fine—
Glares thy impetuous knife, Corday,
  And the lava locks are thine!

I thought of the war-wolves on our trail—
  Their gaunt fangs sluiced with gouts of
    blood—

Till the past, in a dead, mesmeric veil,
    Drooped with its wizard flood;

Till the surly blaze through the iron bars
    Shot to the hearth with a pang and cry,
While a lank howl plunged from the Champs de Mars
    To the Column of July;

Till Corday sprang from the gem, I swear!
    And the dove-eyed damsel I knew had flown;
For Eva was not on the ottoman there,
    By Psyche carved in stone:

She grew like a Pythoness flushed with fate,
    With the incantation in her gaze;
A lip of scorn, an arm of hate,
    And a dirge of the Marseillaise.

Eva, the vision was not wild,
    When wreaked on the tyrants of the land—
For you were transfigured to Nemesis, child,
    With the dagger in your hand!

Melt the Bells.

Melt the bells, melt the bells,
Still the tinkling on the plain,
And transmute the evening chimes
Into war's resounding rhymes,
That the invaders may be slain
          By the bells.

Melt the bells, melt the bells,
That for years have called to prayer,
And instead, the cannon's roar
Shall resound the valleys o'er,
That the foe may catch despair
          From the bells.

Melt the bells, melt the bells,
Though it cost a tear to part
With the music they have made,
Where the ones we loved are laid,
With pale cheek and silent heart,
          'Neath the bells.

Melt the bells, melt the bells,
Into cannon vast and grim,
And the foe shall feel the ire
From its heaving lung of fire,
And we'll put our trust in Him
And the bells.

Melt the bells, melt the bells,
And when the foe is driven back,
And the lightning cloud of war
Shall roll thunderless and far,
We will melt the cannon back
Into bells.

Melt the bells, melt the bells,
And they'll peal a sweeter chime,
And remind of all the brave
Who have sunk to glory's grave,
And will sleep through coming time
'Neath the bells.

Cannon Song.

AHA ! a song for the trumpet's tongue !
  For the bugle to sing before us,
When our gleaming guns, like clarions,
  Shall thunder in battle chorus !
Where the rifles ring, where the bullets sing,
  Where the black bombs whistle o'er us,
With rolling wheel and rattling peal
  They'll thunder in battle chorus !
    With the cannon's flash, and the cannon's crash,
      With the cannon's roar and rattle,
    Let Freedom's sons, with their shouting guns,
      Go down to their country's battle !

Their brassy throats shall learn the notes
  That make old tyrants quiver,
Till the war is done, or each TYRRELL gun,
  Grows cold with our hearts forever !
Where the laurel waves o'er our brothers' graves,
  Who have gone to their rest before us,
Here's a requiem shall sound for them
  And thunder in battle chorus !

With the cannon's flash, and the cannon's crash,
With the cannon's roar and rattle,
Let Freedom's sons, with their shouting guns,
Go down to their country's battle!

By the light that lies in our Southern skies;
! By the spirits that watch above us;
By the gentle hands in our summer lands,
And the gentle hearts that love us!
Our fathers' faith let us keep till death—
Their fame in its cloudless splendor—
As men who stand for their mother land,
And die—but never surrender!
With the cannon's flash, and the cannon's crash,
With the cannon's roar and rattle,
Let Freedom's sons, with their shouting guns,
Go down to their country's battle!

Battle Eve.

I SEE the broad, red, setting sun
   Sink slowly down the sky;
I see—amid the cloud-built tents—
   His blood-red standard fly;
And meek meanwhile, the pallid moon
   Looks from her place on high.

O setting sun, awhile delay!
   Linger on sea and shore;
For thousand eyes now gaze on thee,
   That shall not see thee more;
A thousand hearts beat proudly now,
   Whose race like thine is o'er!

O ghastly moon! thy pallid ray
   On paler brows shall lie!
On many a torn and bleeding heart,
   On many a glazing eye;
And breaking hearts shall live to mourn,
   For whom 'twere bliss to die!

The Unreturning.

THE swallow leaves the ancient eaves,
   As in the days agone;
The wheaten fields are all ablaze
And in and out the west wind plays,
   Amid the tasseled corn.

The sun's rays light as warm and bright
   On clover fields all red;
The wild bird wakes his simple song
As joyfully, the whole day long,
   As if *he* were not dead!

The summer skies, with softest sighs,
   Their rain and sunshine send;
And, standing in the farmhouse door,
I see—dotting the landscape o'er—
   The flocks he used to tend.

The woodbine grows—the jasmine blows—
   Beside the window-sill:
Their soft sweet sigh is in the air,
For the dead hands that placed them there
   On the red field are still.

Around the wolds the summer folds
　　　Her wealth of golden light;
And, past the willows' silvery gleam,
I catch the glimmering of the stream
　　　And lilies, cool and white.

But oh! one shade has solemn made
　　　The sunshine and the bloom;
His voice, whose sweet and gentle words
Were sweeter than the song of birds,
　　　Is silent in the tomb.

How can the day, so bright and gay,
　　　Glare round the farmhouse door?
When all the quiet ways he trod
By leafy wood, or blooming sod,
　　　Shall know him nevermore!

The Last of Earth:

A PRISON SCENE. (xl.)

LAST night a comrade sent in haste
    For me to soothe his fearful pain;
He felt Death's power advancing fast,
    He knew that hope was vain.
God's promises I read again
    Till Faith's sweet light shone from his eye;
Sole gleam—for sorrow filled me then,
    As shadows fill the sky.

A dreary place—that Hospital—
    Where dim lamps break the solemn gloom,
And nurses move with slow footfall,
    Like spectres, through the room.
Above those cots all miseries blend,
    On each some form in suffering lies;
Some groan—some sleep—but here one friend
    Puts on the angel's guise.

Scarcely I heard the bugle's call,
    Scarce felt the night-wind's heavy breath,

I only saw the shadows fall
  And the ghastly chill of death,
Save where a pallid splendor lay
Upon his brow—like Martyr's crown—
The sweet foreshadowing of the Day
  In which Life's star goes down.

I hear his piteous tones implore
  And heed his hand's hot clinging grasp—
Pale hands, alas—that nevermore
  Shall feel Love's answering clasp.
His frenzied spirit flies from pain,
  He thinks himself once more at home:
"Dear wife—dear child—I'm here again,
  Close to me—closer come.

"I could not lag where country led—
  The voice of wrong could not beguile;
You would not have me stay, you said,
  If honor ceased to smile.
Ah! many fall in this wild strife!
  But Freedom holds their memories dear,
And makes a gem of every life—
  For the crown *she* yet shall wear.

"And a many time when raged the fight
   I've seemed to see *her* through the smoke,
With smiles that shone in tearful light,
   Bless every valiant stroke.
I'm hurt and tired now—so place
   Our little darling by my bed;
One hand, my own, to your embrace,
   And one on Baby's head."

His voice was hushed—short grew his breath,
   The glazing eyes closed slowly o'er,
The bloodless lips were kissed by Death—
   They'll speak of love no more.
One clammy hand I held in mine
   And o'er it breathed my fervent prayer—
Beneath the other seemed to shine
   His Baby's golden hair.

The Mother's Trust.

FAR away are our beloved,
  Where resounds the battle-cry;
Where, like hail, the fiery meteors
  Carry death, as on they fly.
Far from home's dear shelter speeding—
  They its joy were wont to be—
God of Battles, safely guide them!
  "*We will trust our boys to Thee!*"

Few the years that each had numbered,
  When they heard their country's call—
When they left the sheltering fireside—
  Home and kindred—left them all.
Vacant is each place, and lonely—
  Must it always vacant be?
Thou—who seest a sparrow falling,
  "*We will trust our boys to Thee!*"

May they, in the hour of danger,
  Say the prayer a mother taught;
May the lessons of their childhood
  With rich blessings now be fraught;

May they never turn, or falter,
   From the path that leads to Thee—
Very precious! in Thy keeping,
   Father, let our children be!

When the strife shall all be ended,
   When the battle shall be won,
May we fondly, proudly greet them,
   Saying—"*Well and bravely done!*"
But, if Thou shouldst early call them,
   Suddenly to breast the tide—
Call them from the midst of battle,
   Sheltered safe at Thy dear side—
May they at their post be watching,
   Ready for the Captain's word,
And, their earthly weapon grounding,
   Be forever with the Lord!
Father, our weak hearts are failing:
   As Thou wilt, so let it be!
'Midst the battle shouldst Thou call them,
   "*We will trust our boys to Thee!*"

And when life's last hour shall find us
   Drifting out upon the tide,
We will breast the chilling waters,
   Knowing *Thou* art close beside.

When we gain the shining shore-side
And the glist'ning portals see,
May *they* be the first to greet us—
Those dear boys we trust to Thee!

A General Invitation.

Come! leave the noisy Longstreet,
    Fly to the Fields with me;
Trip o'er the Heth, with flying feet,
    And skip along the Lee!
There Ewell find the flowers that be
    Along the Stonewall still;
And pluck the buds of flowering pea
    That grow on A. P. Hill.
Across the Rhodes, the Forrest boughs
    A gloomy Archway form,
Where sadly pipes that Early bird
    That never caught the worm!
Come! hasten, for the Bee is gone,
    And Wheat lies on the plains,
And braid a Garland, ere the leaves
    Fall in the *blasting* Rains! (xii.)

The Brave at Home.

THE maid who binds her warrior's sash,
  And smiling, all her pain dissembles—
The while, beneath her drooping lash,
  One starry tear-drop hangs and trembles—
Though Heaven alone records the tear,
  And Fame shall never know her story,
Her heart has shed a drop as dear
  As ever dewed the field of glory!

The wife who girds her husband's sword,
  'Mid little ones who weep and wonder;
And bravely speaks the cheering word,
  What though her heart be rent asunder—
Doomed nightly in her dreams to hear
  The bolts of war around him rattle,
Has shed as sacred blood as e'er
  Was poured upon the field of battle!

The mother who conceals her grief,
  While to her heart her son she presses,
Then breathes a few brave words and brief,
  Kissing the patriot brow she blesses—

With no one but her secret God
   To know the pain that weighs upon her,
Sheds holy blood, as e'er the sod
   Received on Freedom's field of honor!

Maryland.

THE despot's heel is on thy shore,
    Maryland!
His torch is at thy temple door,
    Maryland!
Avenge the patriotic gore
That flecked the streets of Baltimore,
And be the battle-queen of yore,
    Maryland! My Maryland!

Hark to wand'ring son's appeal,
    Maryland!
My mother State! to thee I kneel,
    Maryland!
For life and death, for woe and weal,
Thy peerless chivalry reveal,
And gird thy beauteous limbs with steel,
    Maryland! My Maryland!

Thou wilt not cower in the dust,
    Maryland!
Thy beaming sword shall never rust,
    Maryland!

Remember Carroll's sacred trust;
Remember Howard's warlike thrust,
And all thy Slumberers with the Just,
 Maryland! My Maryland!

Come! 'tis the red dawn of the day,
 Maryland!
Come! with thy panoplied array,
 Maryland!
With Ringgold's spirit for the fray,
With Watson's blood, at Monterey,
With fearless Lowe, and dashing May,
 Maryland! My Maryland!

Dear mother, burst the Tyrant's chain,
 Maryland!
Virginia should not call in vain,
 Maryland!
SHE meets her sisters on the plain,
"*Sic Semper*"—'tis the proud refrain,
That baffles minions back amain,
 Maryland! My Maryland!

Come! for thy shield is bright and strong,
 Maryland!
Come! for thy dalliance does thee wrong,
 Maryland!

Come! to thine own heroic throng,
That stalks with Liberty along,
And ring thy dauntless slogan song,
    Maryland! My Maryland!

I see the blush upon thy cheek,
    Maryland!
For thou wast ever bravely meek,
    Maryland!
But lo! there surges forth a shriek
From hill to hill, from creek to creek—
Potomac calls to Chesapeake,
    Maryland! My Maryland!

Thou wilt not yield the Vandal toll,
    Maryland!
Thou wilt not crook to his control,
    Maryland!
Better the fire upon thee roll,
Better the shot—the blade—the bowl—
Than crucifixion of the soul,
    Maryland! My Maryland!

I hear the distant thunder hum,
    Maryland!
The Old Line bugle, fife and drum,
    Maryland!

She is not dead, nor deaf, nor dumb:
Huzza! she spurns the Northern scum!
She breathes—she burns! she'll come! she'll
    come!
    Maryland! My Maryland!

There's Life in the Old Land yet.

THOUGH the soil of old Maryland echoes the tread
  Of an insolent soldiery now ;
And a lurid glare reddens the sky overhead
  From the camp-fire's light below ;
Though from mountain to shore the hoarse cannon
      roar ;
  And from border to border are sentinels set,
Whose bayonets shine in unbroken line—
  " *There is life in the Old Land yet !* "

Though by treacherous hearts and unloyal hands
  Betrayed and disabled to-day,
And deserted at need by her sons, she stands
  Confronting an armed array ;
Though tyrannous might hath o'erborne the right,
  Hath despoiled and discrowned her — and men
      forget
As they bow the knee, that they once were free—
  " *There is life in the Old Land yet !* "

But though patient and mute, she is still undismayed,
  Though passive, she is not subdued;
Though she shrinks from unsheathing her trusty
    blade
  In a fratricidal feud,
Not long will she kneel when oppression's heel
  On her neck is by monarch, or president set;
And the blood even now is mantling her brow—
  For "there's life in the Old Land yet!"

She remembers with pride what her children have
    done
  In the perilous days of yore,
And will never relinquish the rights which they won,
  Nor disgrace the flag they bore.
Then let those beware, who boastfully swear
  They will conquer her now, for their vaunt will
    be met;
And the Maryland men shall be heard of again—
  For "there's life in the Old Land yet!"

Lines after Defeat.

WE have suffered defeat, as the bravest may suffer;
　Shall we leave unavenged our dead comrades' gore?
Oh! rather, my brothers, rise up in your manhood,
　And strive as no nation e'er battled before.

Come! rush from the mountains, the lowlands, the
　　valleys,
　Rush on like the avalanche freed from its spell;
And lash the base cohorts, that throng to enslave
　　us,
　With stripes that shall give them a foretaste of
　　hell.

Our women, to hearthstone and altar appealing,
　Say — "Shield us from ruin, or die where you
　　stand!"
Our children, O God! can we fondle and bless them,
　While anarchy threatens, while despots command?

No! rise in the strength and the glow of our valor,
　And strike a great blow that shall ring through
　　the world —
A blow that shall shatter our fetters forever,
　And leave our proud banner forever unfurled!

England's Neutrality.

A PARLIAMENTARY DEBATE, WITH NOTES: BY A CONFEDERATE REPORTER.

ALL ye who with credulity the whispers hear of
    fancy,
Or yet pursue with eagerness Hope's wild extrava-
    gancy
Who dream that England soon will drop her long
    miscalled Neutrality,
And give us with a hearty shake, the hand of
    Nationality,

Read, as we give, with little fault of statement or
    omission,
The *next* debate in Parliament on Southern Recog-
    nition;
They're all so much alike, indeed, that one can write
    it off, I see,
As truly as the *Times* report, without the gift of
    prophecy.

Not yet, not yet to interfere does England see
    occasion,
But treats our good Commissioner with coolness
    and evasion ;
Such coolness in the premises that really 'tis refri-
    gerant
To think that two long years ago she called us a
    belligerent.

But further Downing Street is dumb, the Premier
    deaf to reason,
As deaf as is the *Morning Post*, both in and out of
    season ;
The working men of Lancashire are all reduced to
    beggary,
And yet they will not listen unto Roebuck, or to
    Gregory,

" Or any other man," to-day, who counsels interfering,
While all who speak on t'other side obtain a ready
    hearing—
As *par exemple* Mr. Bright, that pink of all propriety,
That meek and mild disciple of the blessed Peace
    Society.

"Why, let 'em fight," says Mr. Bright, "those
 Southerners I hate 'em,
And hope the Black Republicans will soon exter-
 minate 'em;
If Freedom can't Rebellion crush, pray tell me what's
 the use of her?"
And so he chuckles o'er the fray as gleefully as
 Lucifer.

Enough of him; an abler man demands our close
 attention—
The Maximus Apollo of strict *Non-Intervention*.
With pitiless severity, though decorous and calm his
 tone,
Thus speaks the "old man eloquent," the puissant
 Earl of Palmerston:

"What though the land run red with blood; what
 though the lurid flashes
Of cannon-light, at dead of night, a mournful heap
 of ashes,
Where many an ancient mansion stood? what though
 the robber pillages
The sacred home, the house of God, in twice a hundred villages?

"What though a fiendish, nameless wrong that makes
    revenge a duty
Is daily done" (O Lord, how long!) "to tenderness
    and beauty?"—
(And who shall tell, this deed of hell, how deadlier
    far a curse it is
Than even pulling temples down and burning uni-
    versities?)

"Let arts decay, let millions fall, for aye let Freedom
    perish,
With all that in the Western World men fain would
    love and cherish;
Let Universal Ruin there become a sad reality:
We can not swerve, we must preserve our rigorous
    Neutrality."

O, Pam! O, Pam! hast ever read what's writ in
    holy pages,
How blessed the Peace-makers are, God's children
    of the Ages?
Perhaps you think the promise sweet was nothing
    but a platitude;
'Tis clear that *you* have no concern in that divine
    beatitude.

But "hear! hear! hear!" another peer, that mighty
    man of muscle,
Is on his legs, what slender pegs! "ye noble Earl"
    of Russell;
Thus might he speak, did not of speech his shrewd
    reserve the folly see,
And thus unfold the subtle plan of England's secret
    policy:

"John Bright was right! Yes, let 'em fight, these
    fools across the water,
'Tis no affair at all of ours, their carnival of slaughter!
The Christian world, indeed, may say we ought not
    to allow it, sirs,
But still 'tis music in our ears, this roar of Yankee
    howitzers.

"A word or two of sympathy, that costs us not a
    penny,
We give the gallant Southerners, the few against
    the many;
We say their noble fortitude of final triumph pre-
    sages,
And praise in *Blackwood's Magazine* Jeff. Davis
    and his messages—

"Of course we claim the shining fame of glorious
       Stonewall Jackson,
Who typifies the English race, a sterling Anglo-
       Saxon;
To bravest song his deeds belong, to Clio and Mel-
       pomene"—
(And why not for a British stream demand the
       Chickahominy?)

"But for the cause in which he fell we can not lift
       a finger,
'Tis idle on the question any longer here to linger;
'Tis true the South has freely bled, her sorrows are
       Homeric, oh!
Her case is like to his of old who journeyed unto
       Jericho—

"The thieves have stripped and bruised, although
       as yet they have not bound her;
We'd like to see her slay 'em all to right and left
       around her;
We shouldn't cry in Parliament if Lee should cross
       the Raritan,
But England never yet was known to play the Good
       Samaritan.

"And so we pass to t'other side, and leave them to
their glory,
To give new proofs of manliness, new scenes for
song and story;
These honeyed words of compliment may possibly
bamboozle 'em,
But ere we intervene, you know, we'll see 'em in—
Jerusalem.

"Yes, let 'em fight, till both are brought to hope-
less desolation,
Till wolves troop round the cottage door, in one and
t'other nation,
Till, worn and broken down, the South shall prove
no more refractory,
And rust eats up the silent looms of every Yankee
factory—

"Till bursts no more the cotton boll o'er fields of
Carolina,
And fills with snowy flosses the dusky hands of
Dinah;
Till War has dealt its final blow, and Mr. Seward's
knavery
Has put an end in all the land to Freedom and to
Slavery:

"The grim Bastille, the rack, the wheel, without
remorse or pity,
May flourish with the guillotine in every Yankee
city,
No matter should Old Abe revive the brazen bull of
Phalaris,
'Tis no concern at all of ours"—(sensation in the
galleries.)

"So shall our 'merrie England' thrive on trans-
Atlantic troubles,
While India on her distant plains her crop of cotton
doubles;
And so as long as North or South shall show the
least vitality,
We can not swerve, we must preserve our rigorous
Neutrality."

Your speech, my lord, might well become a Saxon
legislator,
When the "fine old English gentleman" lived in a
state of natur',
When vikings quaffed from human skulls their fiery
draughts of honey mead,
Long, long before the barons bold met tyrant John
at Runnymede—

But 'tis a speech so plain, my lord, that all may
    understand it,
And so we quickly turn again to fight the Yankee
    bandit,
Convinced that we shall fairly win at last our
    nationality,
Without the help of Britain's arm—*in spite of* her
    Neutrality.

The Fancy Shot. (xiii.)

"Rifleman, shoot me a fancy shot,
 Straight at the heart of yon prowling vidette;
Ring me a ball on the glittering spot,
 That shines on his breast like an amulet!"

"Ah! Captain, here goes for a fine-drawn bead;
 There's music around, when my barrel's in tune."
Crack! went the rifle, the messenger sped,
 And dead from his horse fell the ringing dragoon.

"Now, rifleman, steal through the bushes, and snatch
 From your victim some trinket to handsel first
   blood;
A button, a loop, or that luminous patch,
 That gleams in the moon like a diamond stud."

.   .   .   .

"O Captain! I staggered and sunk in my track,
 When I gazed on the face of the fallen vidette;
For he looked so like you as he lay on his back,
 That my heart rose upon me and masters me yet.

" But I snatched off the trinket—this locket of
　　gold—
An inch from the centre my lead broke its way,
Scarce grazing the picture, so fair to behold,
　　Of a beautiful lady in bridal array."

"Ha! rifleman, fling me the locket—'tis she!
　My brother's young bride—and the fallen dragoon
Was her husband—hush! soldier, 'twas heaven's
　　decree;
　We must bury him there by the light of the moon!

"But hark! the far bugles their warning unite;
　War is a virtue, weakness a sin.
There's lurking and loping around us to-night:
　Load again, rifleman—keep your hand in!"

Volunteered.

I KNOW the sun shines, and the lilacs are blowing,
  And the summer sends kisses by beautiful May.
Oh! to see the rich treasures the spring is bestow-
      ing,
  And think—my boy, WILLIE, enlisted to-day!

It seems but a day since, at twilight, low humming,
  I rocked him to sleep with his cheek upon mine;
While ROBBY, the four-year-old, watched for the
      coming
  Of father adown the street's indistinct line.

It is many a year since my HARRY departed
  To come back no more, in the twilight, or dawn;
And ROBBY grew weary of watching, and started
  Alone on the journey his father had gone.

It is many a year; and this afternoon, sitting
  At ROBBY's old window, I heard the band play,
And quickly ceased dreaming over my knitting,
  To recollect—WILLIE is twenty to-day!

And that, standing beside him this soft May-day
    morning,
The sun making gold of his wreathed cigar smoke—
I saw in his sweet eye and lip a faint warning,
    And choked down the tears when he eagerly spoke.

"Dear mother, you know how these Northmen are
    crowing—
They would trample the rights of the South in the
    dust;
The boys are all fire; and they wish I were going—"
    He stopped, but his eyes said—"Oh! say if I must!"

I smiled on the boy, though my heart it seemed
    breaking;
My eyes filled with tears—but I turned them away;
And I answered him—"WILLIE, 'tis well you are
    waking—
Go! act as your father would bid you to-day!"

I sit in the window and see the flags flying,
    And dreamily list to the roll of the drum;
And smother the pain in my heart that is lying,
    And bid all the fears in my bosom be dumb.

I shall sit in the window, when summer is lying
  Out over the fields, and the honey bee's hum
Lulls the rose at the porch from her tremulous sigh-
      ing,
  And watch for the face of my darling to come.

And, if he should fall—his young life he has given
  For Freedom's sweet sake; and for me—I will pray
Once more with my HARRY and ROBBY, in Heaven,
  To meet the dear boy, that enlisted to-day.

John Pelham.

JUST as the spring came laughing through the
strife,
    With all its gorgeous cheer;—
In the glad April of historic life—
    Fell the great cannoneer!

The wondrous lulling of a hero's breath
    His bleeding country weeps;
Hushed—in the alabaster arms of Death—
    Our young Marcellus sleeps.

Grander and nobler than the child of Rome,
    Curbing his chariot steeds,
The knightly scion of a Southern home
    Dazzled the land with deeds!

Gentlest and bravest in the battle's brunt—
    The Champion of the Truth—
He bore his banner to the very front
    Of our immortal youth!

A clang of sabres 'mid Virginia's snow,
    The fiery pang of shells—
And there's a wail of immemorial woe
    In Alabama dells:

The pennon droops, that led the sacred band
    Along the crimson field;
The meteor blade sinks from the nerveless hand,
    Over the spotless shield!

We gazed and gazed upon that beauteous face,
    While, round the lips and eyes,
Couched in their marble slumber, flashed the
        grace
    Of a divine surprise.

Oh, mother of a blessèd soul on high,
    Thy tears may soon be shed!
Think of thy boy, with Princes of the sky,
    Among the Southern dead!

How must he smile on this dull world beneath,
    Fevered with swift renown—
He, with the martyr's amaranthine wreath,
    Twining the victor's crown!

The Obsequies of Stuart.

WE could not pause, while yet the noontide air
  Shook with the cannonade's incessant pealing,
The funeral pageant fitly to prepare—
  A nation's grief revealing.

The smoke, above the glimmering woodland wide
  That skirts our southward border, in its beauty,
Marked where our heroes stood and fought and died
  For love and faith and duty.

And still, what time the doubtful strife went on,
  We might not find expression for our sorrow;
We could but lay our dear, dumb warrior down,
  And gird us for the morrow.

One weary year agone, when came a lull,
  With victory, in the conflict's stormy closes,
When the glad Spring, all flushed and beautiful,
  First mocked us with her roses—

With dirge and bell and minute gun, we paid
  Some few poor rites—an inexpressive token
Of a great people's pain—to JACKSON's shade,
  In agony unspoken.

No wailing trumpet and no tolling bell,
    No cannon, save the battle's boom receding,
When STUART to the grave we bore might tell,
    With hearts all crushed and bleeding.

The crisis suited not with pomp, and she,
    Whose anguish bears the seal of consecration,
Had wished his Christian obsequies should be
    Thus void of ostentation.

Only the maidens came, sweet flow'rs to twine
    Above his form so still and cold and painless,
Whose deeds upon our brightest record shine,
    Whose life and sword were stainless.

They well remembered how he loved to dash
    Into the fight, festooned from summer bowers;
How like a fountain's spray his sabre's flash
    Leaped from a mass of flowers.

And so we carried to his place of rest
    All that of our great Paladin was mortal;
The cross, and not the sabre, on his breast,
    That opes the heavenly portal.

No more of tribute might to us remain—
  But there will come a time when Freedom's martyrs
A richer guerdon of renown shall gain,
  Than gleams in stars and garters.

I claim no prophet's vision, but I see
  Through coming years—now near at hand, now
      distant—
My rescued country, glorious and free,
  And strong and self-existent.

I hear from out that sunlit land, which lies
  Beyond these clouds that gather darkly o'er us,
The happy sounds of industry arise
  In swelling, peaceful chorus.

And, mingling with these sounds, the glad acclaim
  Of millions, undisturbed by war's afflictions,
Crowning each martyr's never-dying name
  With grateful benedictions.

In some fair future garden of delights,
  Where flowers shall bloom and song-birds sweetly
      warble,
Art shall erect the statues of our knights
  In living bronze and marble:

And none of all that bright, heroic throng,
  Shall wear to far-off time a semblance grander—
Shall still be decked with fresher wreaths of song,
  Than this beloved commander.

The Spanish legend tells us of the Cid,
  That after death he rode erect, sedately,
Along his lines, even as in life he did,
  In presence yet more stately:

And thus our STUART, at this moment, seems
  To ride out of our dark and troubled story
Into the region of romance and dreams,
  A realm of light and glory—

And sometimes, when the silver bugles blow,
  That ghostly form, in battle re-appearing,
Shall lead his horsemen headlong on the foe,
  In victory careering!

Is there any News of the War?

"Is there any news of the war?" she said.
"Only a list of the wounded and dead,"
  Was the man's reply, without raising his eye
  To the face of the woman standing by.
"'Tis the very thing I wish," she said—
"Read me a list of the wounded and dead."

He read her the list; 'twas a long array
Of the wounded and slain on that fatal day.
  In the very midst was a pause, to tell
  Of a gallant youth who fought so well,
  That his comrades asked, "Who is he, pray?"
"The only son of the Widow Gray,"
  Was the proud reply of his Captain nigh.

"Well, well, read on.　Is he wounded?—quick!
  O God! but my heart is sorrow-sick!"
  And the man replied—"Is he wounded? Nay,
  He was *killed outright* in that fatal fray."
  But see! the woman has swooned away.

Slowly she opened her eyes to the light,
Faintly she murmured, "Killed outright!
Alas, and he was my only son;
But the will of the Lord, let it be done!"
God pity the cheerless Widow Gray,
And the light of His peace illumine her way!

A Prayer for Peace.

Peace! Peace! God of our fathers, grant us Peace!
Unto our cry of anguish and despair
Give ear and pity! From the lonely homes,
Where widowed beggary and orphaned woe
Fill their poor urns with tears; from trampled plains,
Where the bright harvest Thou hast sent us rots—
The blood of them, who should have garnered it,
Calling to Thee—from fields of carnage, where
The foul-beaked vultures, sated, flap their wings
O'er crowded corpses, that but yesterday
Bore hearts of brothers, beating high with love
And common hopes and pride; all blasted now—
Father of Mercies! not alone from these
Our prayer and wail are lifted. Not alone
Upon the battle's seared and desolate track,
Nor with the sword and flame, is it, O God!
That Thou hast smitten us. Around our hearths,
And in the crowded streets and busy marts,
Where echo whispers not the far-off strife
That slays our loved ones; in the solemn halls
Of safe and quiet counsel—nay, beneath
The temple-roofs that we have reared to Thee,

And 'mid their rising incense, God of Peace!
The curse of war is on us. Greed and hate,
Hungering for gold and blood: Ambition, bred
Of passionate vanity and sordid lusts,
Mad with the base desire of tyrannous sway
Over men's souls and thoughts, have set their price
On human hecatombs, and sell and buy
Their sons and brothers for the shambles. Priests,
With white, anointed, supplicating hands,
From Sabbath unto Sabbath clasped to Thee,
Burn, in their tingling pulses, to fling down
Thy censers and Thy cross to clutch the throats
Of kinsmen by whose cradles they were born,
Or grasp the brand of Herod, and go forth
Till Rachel hath no children left to slay.
The very name of Jesus, writ upon
Thy shrines, beneath the spotless, outstretched wings
Of Thine Almighty Dove, is wrapt and hid
With bloody battle-flags, and from the spires
That rise above them, angry banners flout
The skies to which they point, amid the clang
Of rolling war-songs, tuned to mock Thy praise.

All things once prized and honored are forgot.
The Freedom that we worshiped, next to Thee;

The manhood that was Freedom's spear and shield;
The proud, true heart; the brave, out-spoken word,
Which might be stifled, but could never wear
The guise, whate'er the profit, of a lie—
All these are gone, and in their stead, have come
The vices of the miser and the slave,
Scorning no shame that bringeth gold or power,
Knowing no love, or faith, or reverence,
Or sympathy, or tie, or aim, or hope,
Save as begun in self, and ending there.
With vipers like to these, O blessed God!
Scourge us no longer! Send us down, once more,
Some shining seraph in Thy glory clad,
To wake the midnight of our sorrowing
With tidings of Good Will and Peace to men:
And if the star that through the darkness led
Earth's wisdom then, guide not our folly now!
Oh, be the lightning Thine Evangelist,
With all its fiery, forkèd tongues, to speak
The unanswerable message of Thy will.

Peace! Peace! God of our fathers, grant us Peace!
Peace in our hearts and at Thine altars; Peace
On the red waters and their blighted shores;
Peace for the leaguered cities, and the hosts

That watch and bleed, around them and within;
Peace for the homeless and the fatherless;
Peace for the captive on his weary way,
And the mad crowds who jeer his helplessness.
For them that suffer, them that do the wrong;
Sinning and sinned against—O God! for all—
For a distracted, torn, and bleeding land—
Speed the glad tidings! Give us, give us Peace!

⋅The Conquered Banner.

FURL that banner, for 'tis weary;
Round its staff 'tis drooping dreary.
    Furl it—fold it: it is best;
For there's not a man to wave it,
And there's not a sword to save it;
There's not one left to lave it
In the blood that heroes gave it;
And its foes now scorn and brave it!
    Furl it—fold it; let it rest!

Take that banner down! 'Tis tattered!
Broken is its staff and shattered;
And the valiant hosts are scattered,
    Over whom it floated high.
Oh! 'tis hard for us to fold it—
Hard to think there's none to hold it!
And that those, who once unrolled it,
    Now must furl it with a sigh!

Furl that banner! Furl it sadly!
Once, six millions hailed it gladly,
And ten thousands wildly, madly,
    Swore it should forever wave!

Swore that foeman's sword should never
Hearts entwined like theirs dissever—
And, upheld by brave endeavor,
That dear flag should float forever
   O'er their freedom or their grave.

Furl it! For the hands that grasped it,
And the hearts that fondly clasped it,
   Cold and dead are lying low:
And that banner prone is trailing,
While around it sounds the wailing
   Of its people in their woe!
For, though conquered, they adore it;
Love the cold, dead hands that bore it:
Weep for those who fell before it—
Pardon those who trailed and tore it—
And, oh! wildly they deplore it,
   Now to furl and fold it so!

Furl that banner! True, 'tis gory;
Yet 'tis wreathed around with glory,
And 'twill live in song and story,
   Though now prostrate in the dust!
For its fame, on brightest pages
Penned by poets and by sages,
Shall go sounding down the ages,
   Furl its folds though now we must!

Furl that banner! sadly—slowly!
Treat it gently—it is holy,
    For it waves above the dead.
Touch it not—unfurl it never!
Let it lie there, furled forever—
    For its people's hopes are dead!

NOTES.

NOTES.

Note I.—"YOUR MISSION."

I AM not perfectly certain of the authorship of this poem. It appeared anonymously in a Charleston newspaper, and was never claimed by its modest author. In the South it was variously attributed to Mrs. Browning, J. R. Thompson, Mrs. Preston, and Paul Hayne. I am sure that neither of the three last wrote it; and the credit was given to the first because of the combined strength and pathos of the poem, and its applicability to the war in Italy. I do not think either reason strong enough to warrant the belief; and while I desire to pluck no leaf from the wreath that will to all time adorn the brow of THE GRAND WOMAN, I still think some "mute inglorious Milton" from the South will yet place himself in the goodly company of the poets by acknowledging its authorship.

Note II.—THE BURIAL OF LATANE

is only a metrical narration of facts, as they occurred. In General Jeb Stuart's celebrated tour to the White House, round the rear of McClellan's army—known as the PAMUNKEY

RAID—Captain Latané was killed in a skirmish. The follow-
ing extract from a private letter to Mr. Thompson, from a lady
who was present, tells the story in better language than any I
can use: "Lieutenant Latané carried his brother's dead body
to Mrs. Brockenbrough's plantation, an hour or two after his
death. On this sad and lonely errand he met a party of
Yankees, who followed him to Mrs. Brockenbrough's gate,
and stopping there, told him that as soon as he had placed
his brother's body in friendly hands, he must surrender himself prisoner. . . . . Mrs. Brockenbrough sent for an
Episcopal clergyman to perform the funeral ceremonies, but
the enemy would not permit him to pass. Then, with a few
other ladies, a fair-haired little girl, her apron filled with white
flowers, and a few faithful slaves, who stood reverently near, a
pious Virginia matron read the solemn and beautiful Burial
Service over the cold, still form of one of the noblest gentle-
men and most intrepid officers in the Confederate army. She
watched the sods heaped upon the coffin-lid, then sinking on
her knees, in sight and hearing of the foe, she committed his
soul's welfare, and the stricken hearts he had left behind him,
to the mercy of the 'All-Father.' "

Note III.—THE LONE SENTRY.

The anecdote of Napoleon keeping post to reprove a sleep-
ing sentinel was changed by General Jackson to fit the
mould of his grander soul. When his brigade came up to
Manassas, the men were so worn down by the toilsome march

that they threw themselves on the ground, and without eating even, slept as they fell. The Adjutant, in speaking of a picket detail, mentioned their condition. "*No!*" said the noble Jackson, "*Let them sleep, and I will watch the camp to-night.*"

Note IV.—A POEM THAT NEEDS NO DEDICATION.

The incident suggesting this poem—the burning of Luna by the sea-robber, Hasting—is to be found in Milman's History of Latin Christianity. Its applicability I leave to the reader.

Note V.—"THERE'S LIFE IN THE OLD LAND YET."

In a recent letter Mr. Randall informs me that it was not until this poem had been written several months that he saw Massey's " *Old England,*" in which a similar refrain occurs. Mr. Howard has ably used the same theme.

Note VI.—"THE WAR CHRISTIAN'S THANKSGIVING"

was written on the occasion of a governmental thanksgiving-day, about the end of '63. It was never published except on slips for local distribution; and even that was done before the author himself was apprised of it.

Note VII.—A WORD WITH THE WEST

was published in Richmond on the occasion of General J. E. Johnston's leaving to take command of the Western Department at the end of 1862.

Note VIII.—"NEWLY WROUGHT IN THE FORGES OF SPAIN."

A magnificent Toledo blade, bearing the mark of the royal manufactory, had just been brought from Spain, and presented to General Johnston by a gentleman of Alabama.

Note IX.—"MURMUROUS PINES."

General Johnston was the commander of the Virginia army at the "*Battle of Seven Pines*," and gained much honor with the people of the State for his conduct of the affair. He was badly wounded on the first day, when the command devolved upon General R. E. Lee.

Note X.—BEAUREGARD'S APPEAL

was for the *plantation bells only* to melt into cannon; but at once numbers of the churches offered theirs. Some of these latter that were accepted and not used, have recently been returned to their owners by the United States officers.

The sister poem to this, called forth by the same proclamation, was never acknowledged. It has a ring and fire that make it somewhat remarkable that this modest but valuable contribution to the bell-fund was never placed at the right door.

Note XI.—A PRISON SCENE,

as well as the touching poem by the same author that precedes it, was written while Colonel Hawkins was a prisoner of war at Camp Chase. After a long and wearing imprisonment, the close of the war liberated him, only to see his "fair, sunny land" and die. But he will not be forgotten as long as his people love the poetry of true feeling.

Note XII.—"FALL IN THE BLASTING RAINS."

General Rains had charge of the torpedo and pyrotechnic department of the army.

Note XIII.—THE FANCY SHOT

has been claimed as a Northern poem. It was first *published* in ONCE A WEEK, as English property, but manuscript copies had for some time been in circulation in the South.

It is no strained image of the horrors of the civil war that the poem presents.